TAEKWONDO FOR ALL

GLIMPSES OF WORLD'S NO. 1 MARTIAL ART

Sai R

Chennai • Bangalore

CLEVER FOX PUBLISHING
Chennai, India

Published by CLEVER FOX PUBLISHING 2024
Copyright © Sai R 2024

All Rights Reserved.
ISBN: 978-93-67079-51-5

This book has been published with all reasonable efforts taken to make the material error-free after the consent of the author. No part of this book shall be used, reproduced in any manner whatsoever without written permission from the author, except in the case of brief quotations embodied in critical articles and reviews.

The Author of this book is solely responsible and liable for its content including but not limited to the views, representations, descriptions, statements, information, opinions and references ["Content"]. The Content of this book shall not constitute or be construed or deemed to reflect the opinion or expression of the Publisher or Editor. Neither the Publisher nor Editor endorse or approve the Content of this book or guarantee the reliability, accuracy or completeness of the Content published herein and do not make any representations or warranties of any kind, express or implied, including but not limited to the implied warranties of merchantability, fitness for a particular purpose. The Publisher and Editor shall not be liable whatsoever for any errors, omissions, whether such errors or omissions result from negligence, accident, or any other cause or claims for loss or damages of any kind, including without limitation, indirect or consequential loss or damage arising out of use, inability to use, or about the reliability, accuracy or sufficiency of the information contained in this book.

Dedication

To the coaches all over the world who inspire, motivate, and shape lives through the power of their guidance and dedication, this book is dedicated to you!

Contents

About the Author .... *vii*
Preface .... *ix*

Chapter 1. Taekwondo and Me 1
Chapter 2. History of Taekwondo 8
Chapter 3. Organization 12
Chapter 4. Features and Philosophy of Taekwondo 16
Chapter 5. Basic Taekwondo Vocabulary 21
Chapter 6. Poomsae 30
Chapter 7. Kyorugi 48
Chapter 8. Neel's Taekwondo Diary 59

About the Author
SAI

Sai is an accomplished Indian writer and Taekwondo coach with a deep passion for martial arts. With a rich background in multiple disciplines, Sai holds a 3rd Dan Black Belt in Taekwondo and a 1st Dan Black Belt in Thang Ta.

About the Author

Sai's love for the written word and deep understanding of the transformative power of martial arts led him to pursue a career as a writer. Drawing upon his extensive experience in training and coaching, Sai's work aims to inspire and educate readers, guiding them on a journey of self-discovery through the world of Taekwondo.

As the founder of Rajmata Taekwondo Academy, Sai has trained hundreds of students in Taekwondo. He is dedicated to sharing his knowledge and expertise with students of all ages and skill levels.

Through his writing and coaching, Sai hopes to inspire individuals to embrace martial arts as a path to personal growth, empowerment, and self-discovery. He invites readers and students alike to discover the transformative potential within themselves and embark on a remarkable journey of physical, mental, and spiritual development through the art of Taekwondo.

Preface

Welcome to the captivating world of Taekwondo! Whether you are a beginner seeking to embark on a new martial arts journey or an experienced practitioner looking to deepen your understanding, this book is designed to accompany you on your path.

Taekwondo is more than just a combat sport; it is a way of life. Derived from ancient Korean martial arts, it embodies a rich history, a set of values, and a transformative philosophy. It is a discipline that not only hones physical prowess but also nurtures mental strength and emotional well-being. Through this book, I aim to reveal the essence of Taekwondo and equip you with knowledge that extends beyond the realm of physical fighting.

In the following chapters, we will explore the fundamental principles of Taekwondo, such as the importance of respect, discipline, and perseverance. I will guide you through various forms and patterns, detailing their significance and practice drills to help you perfect your execution.

This book is not only intended for those who have already devoted themselves to the art of Taekwondo, but also for those who are curious and open-minded. It is my belief that anyone can benefit from the wisdom that stems from martial arts training, regardless of age or ability.

Taekwondo offers a means for personal growth, self-discovery, and the development of resilience, and my hope is that this book will ignite that spark within you.

As a practitioner and instructor, I have been fortunate enough to witness the transformative power of Taekwondo firsthand. Through this book, my goal is to share my passion and knowledge with you, to inspire and empower you on your own Taekwondo journey. Whether you seek physical fitness, mental clarity, self-defense skills, or a deeper connection to yourself and others, Taekwondo can offer you a pathway to fulfill these aspirations.

I encourage you to approach this book with an open mind and heart, embracing the challenges and embracing the growth that Taekwondo brings. May this guide serve as a source of inspiration, motivation, and guidance, as we embark on this remarkable journey together.

Let us now take the first step on the path to discovering the art of Taekwondo!

Best regards,

SAI

Chapter 1

TAEKWONDO AND ME

Hello friends, welcome! Today we are going to talk about Taekwondo, a martial art that has become very popular around the world. If you are reading this, it means that you are either an avid student of Taekwondo or have a desire to learn more about it. I assure you that this book will not disappoint you. Through this book, we will explore all the fundamental aspects of Taekwondo in detail. This book is a combination of my personal experience, study, and discussions with many Taekwondo coaches. Although this book cannot replace your coach, I believe it can become your guide and friend.

First of all, let me share with you what Taekwondo means to me and how it has impacted my life. I started practicing Taekwondo when I was 20 years old. Growing up in a small village, we didn't have any facilities for technical training in Taekwondo or any other sport. It was only when I moved to a hostel for college that I stumbled upon Taekwondo by accident. I watched children practicing Taekwondo in the front ground and got curious. When I asked the coach if he would teach us, he agreed to teach a group of us. His name is Rajan Luwang, a 4th Dan Black Belt from South Korea.

At first, I practiced Taekwondo only as a martial art because I had never heard of it before. However, as time went by, my coach introduced me to the world of Taekwondo. I had many questions about Taekwondo, and my coach did his best to answer them all. However, hundreds of questions remained unanswered. I looked for answers on the internet, but the information was not in a certain format, making it difficult to understand. I realized that there should be a guide for Taekwondo like other subjects, so that I could get answers to my questions whenever I needed them. When I started my own Taekwondo academy, I noticed that my students had the same questions as I did, but not everyone asked. That's why I decided to write a book about Taekwondo that is simple, easy, and relaxing to read.

This book is divided into eight chapters to provide a comprehensive understanding of Taekwondo. It's designed to be helpful for those who want to learn Taekwondo but may have doubts or fears, as well as for students and coaches of Taekwondo. Chapters one and eight are specifically tailored for those who do not practice Taekwondo but are interested in learning it. The aim is to spark curiosity and encourage everyone to try and learn Taekwondo. Before delving into Taekwondo, it's important to understand what martial arts is and dispel any misconceptions. Many people have a false perception of martial arts derived from movies. However, what is shown in the movies is not even close to what martial arts truly are. There are over 150 different types of martial arts in the world, each with its own unique techniques and origin. Taekwondo is from South Korea, Karate is from Japan, Muay Thai is from Thailand, and Kung Fu is from China. Traditional martial arts such as Mardani Khel, Malla Yudh, Kalaripayattu, Thang-Ta, Adimurai, and Gatka are practiced in India. Each martial art has a significant influence on the culture and lives of the people in their respective areas. The techniques used in each martial art are different. For instance, Taekwondo uses different punching and kicking techniques from Muay Thai, while boxing has its unique punching techniques. On the other hand, wrestling aims to defeat the opponent by grappling without using punches or kicks. Therefore, it's essential to understand that all martial arts are not the same, and there's a vast difference in their techniques.

Many people believe that you need to be physically fit to learn taekwondo, but this is a false assumption. Even if you do not participate in other sports or activities, you can start practicing taekwondo. In fact, those who are not involved in any other sport tend to learn taekwondo faster because their minds are clearer. People who play multiple sports often get confused over small cues. Therefore, you can join taekwondo even if you are not fit and have not exercised before. In some cases, people may feel hesitant to join a taekwondo class because they believe they need to be fit, but this is not true. Many people join taekwondo to lose weight, but they may feel intimidated when they see everyone in the class is already fit. However, most students in a taekwondo class become fit after consistent practice. No sport or type of exercise will give you instant results, but if you are disciplined and consistent in your practice, you will begin to notice changes in your body quickly. If your body feels sore after starting the exercise, you need to inform your trainer so that they can give you proper instructions. With consistent practice, you will feel energetic and confident in as little as one month.

Another common misconception about taekwondo is that it should be started at a young age. However, this is not true either. There is no age limit for learning taekwondo. In fact, the oldest black belt student in my academy is 30 years old, and I started practicing taekwondo when I was 20. Learning something new has nothing to do with age. As the saying goes, "The best time to plant a tree was 20 years ago. The second-best time is now." There is nothing wrong with starting to learn taekwondo at any age. Starting taekwondo at a young age has some advantages, such as greater flexibility and stamina, but starting at an older age also has its benefits. After the age of 25, people often become busy with jobs, businesses, and family responsibilities, but this should not be a reason to avoid learning something new. In fact, people who have no desire to learn often use these reasons as an excuse. Learning any art form, such as taekwondo, can make life meaningful and enjoyable. While physical ability may decrease with age, it can be cultivated with hard work, discipline, perseverance, and patience. Once physical abilities increase, life becomes more enjoyable, and we feel healthier and more confident. So, why not start learning taekwondo today?

There is a common misconception that Taekwondo is all about fighting. But this is not true. You may join Taekwondo for various reasons such as exercise, weight loss, self-defense, or just for fun. Participating in competitions or matches is optional and entirely up to you. Some people join Taekwondo just for playing fights and then continue it as a hobby or exercise. On the other hand, some join it as an exercise and then participate in various competitions. It is essential to understand that everyone has different preferences and abilities. You don't have to compete just because others in your class do so. Find your own reasons for practicing Taekwondo, and only then it can bring you joy.

It is also a common misconception that all martial arts are violent. This idea is mainly due to media and social media, which often only show the violent or attractive moves. However, martial arts offer many qualities such as practice, fitness, mind game, concentration, and patience that are often neglected. Parents should also take some responsibility by recognizing that children often play violent video games where they shoot their enemies, and this is more violent than any martial arts. Some martial arts classes may also deviate from their original purpose and focus on attractive things such as breaking bricks with head or walking through fire. However, these things have nothing to do with martial arts. Teachers have a responsibility to convey the spiritual, artistic, and health aspects of Taekwondo to students and parents. Parents should avoid martial arts classes that do not focus on self-development and overall development of the students. It is not difficult to find the right class if parents do some research. The purpose of Taekwondo is not violence. It has many mental and physical benefits such as increasing concentration, self-confidence, self-awareness, and body strength. Practicing Taekwondo can also help balance weight, improve self-defense, and increase body energy. It is crucial to understand that violence cannot bring satisfaction or medals. As Shifu Yan Lei said, "The purpose of all our training is to find peace within ourselves."

Dear friends, I want to clear up all misconceptions or answer any questions you may have about taekwondo. I understand that many of you reading this book are learning the martial art, while others may be considering it. For those who do not have access to taekwondo classes, I encourage you to explore other forms of traditional martial arts. It is important to note that every country and society in the world has its own form of martial art. In fact, in the past, learning a martial art was almost compulsory. But nowadays, we are moving away from these traditions due to our changing lifestyles, despite the physical and mental benefits they can provide. I believe everyone should learn some form of martial art, and since this book focuses on taekwondo, let's examine some reasons why you should learn it. Firstly, taekwondo takes less time to master compared to other martial arts. While it can take up to 5-6 years to earn a black belt in other forms, with regular practice, you can achieve a black belt in taekwondo in just 2.5-3 years. This makes it an attractive option for those with time constraints. In addition, the taekwondo dress and moves are cool and classy! Another compelling reason to learn taekwondo is that it is an Olympic sport. The Olympic Medal is the highest honor one can receive in the world of sports, making taekwondo an ideal choice for parents who want their children to pursue sports as a career or for students who are interested in the field of sports. Moreover, taekwondo is a less expensive option compared to other sports. Practicing taekwondo requires only a free space, and no expensive courts or equipment. For those who practice taekwondo but want to pursue a career in another field, the certificate earned from competing at the state or national level can be useful in other areas. For instance, sports quota is available in every government college for admission or government jobs. There are countless reasons to learn taekwondo, so find your reason and start learning today! If you encounter any problems while learning, your coach and this book are here to help you. If you have any questions, please discuss them with your coach, who can help you overcome any hurdles you may face. Remember, taekwondo will not only teach you the martial art but also how to face challenges in life. Happy learning!

My Notes

Chapter 2

HISTORY OF TAEKWONDO

The oldest kinds of Korean martial arts were developed by the three rival Korean Kingdoms of Goguryeo, Silla, and Baekje. These techniques were a mash-up of unarmed combat styles, the most popular of which were ssireum, subak, and taekkyon.

However, martial arts were discouraged and restricted to military use throughout the late Joseon dynasty. As a result, Korean martial arts fell out of favor in society. Taekkyon was still taught as a professional military martial art throughout Joseon until the 19th century as a folk game at the May-Dano festival.

Following the end of World War II and the Japanese occupation in 1945, new martial arts schools known as kwans sprouted up in Seoul. Korean martial artists with roots in Chinese and Japanese martial arts founded these schools. Taekkyon was one of the indigenous arts that was being neglected at the time due to years of forced Japanization by the Japanese colonial administration.

It was possible for the founders of the original nine kwans to study judo, kendo, and other Japanese martial arts in Japan. Others were introduced to the native Korean martial art of taekkyon as well as the martial arts of China and Manchuria. Traditionalism and revisionism are the two primary schools of thought that have been discussed in discussions regarding the historical influences of taekwondo. Revisionism, the dominant theory, contends that Taekwondo originated in Karate, whereas traditionalism maintains that Taekwondo has native roots. In an effort to provide Korea with a "Legitimate Cultural Past," traditionalist viewpoints have received substantial backing from the Korean government. President Syngman Rhee of South Korea witnessed a martial arts exhibition in 1952 by officers from the 29th Infantry Division of the South Korean Army, Choi Hong-hi and Nam Tae-hi. But he incorrectly recognized the demonstration method as taekkyon and advocated for the army to adopt a unified system for martial arts.

Leaders of Korea's "kwans," or multiple martial arts schools, began debating the prospect of uniting their talents to form a single martial art in 1955. Korean karate was referred to as "Tang Soo Do" before. A unified style of Korean martial arts was also referred to as "Tae Soo Do". To integrate Korean martial arts under a single system, the Korea Tang Soo Do Association (KTA) was founded in 1959 and eventually changed its name to the Korea Taekwondo Association (KTA). Some kwans refused to accept Choi Hong-hi, the KTA's founder, who insisted that all member kwans learn his Chan Hon form of taekwondo. Instead, they preferred a single style that combined the history and best aspects of all styles. Choi Hong-hi promoted the adoption of the term "Tae Kwon Do," substituting the hanja character "fist" (kwon) and the character "hand" (su). The name was also the closest to how "taekkyon" was pronounced. However, the new name took some time to catch on among the Kwan leaders. Taekwondo was also adopted for use by the South Korean military at this time, which increased its popularity among civilian martial arts schools.

In response to the opposition, Choi Hong-hi left the KTA in 1966 to found the International Taekwon-Do Federation (ITF) in Canada, which was dedicated to establishing his Chan Hon-style of taekwondo. Because of his personal relationship with Choi, the South Korean president initially supported the ITF, but the two eventually split over the issue of North Korean influence in martial arts. South Korea withdrew its support for the ITF in 1972, but it continued to operate independently from its headquarters in Toronto, Canada. Choi continued to refine the ITF style, culminating in the release of his Encyclopedia of Taekwon-Do in 1983. In 2001 and 2002, the ITF split into three separate federations, all operating under the same name.

The KTA and the South Korean Ministry of Culture, Sports, and Tourism established the Kukkiwon as the new national taekwondo academy in 1972. Kukkiwon now performs many of the KTA's previous functions, defining a government-sponsored unified style of taekwondo. The KTA and Kukkiwon supported the formation of the World Taekwondo Federation (WTF) in 1973, which later changed its name to "World Taekwondo" (WT) to avoid confusion with an internet slang term. The Kukkiwon emphasizes the martial art and self-defense aspects of Kukki-Taekwondo, whereas the WT emphasizes the sporting aspect, with competitions employing a subset of Kukkiwon-style Taekwondo techniques. Kukkiwon-style Taekwondo is also known as WT-style Taekwondo, sport-style Taekwondo, or Olympic-style Taekwondo, but the Kukkiwon, not the WT, defines the style.

Taekwondo, along with judo, karate, Greco-Roman wrestling, freestyle wrestling, and boxing, has been one of six martial arts included in the Olympic Games since 2021. A year after becoming a medal event at the Pan American Games, it became a demonstration event at the 1988 games in Seoul. It was designated as an official medal event at the 2000 Sydney Olympics and was accepted as a Commonwealth Games sport in 2010.

My Notes

Chapter 3

ORGANIZATION

WT (World Taekwondo)

World Taekwondo (WT) is the governing body for the sport of Taekwondo and is a member of the Association of Summer Olympic International Federations (ASOIF) and the International Paralympic Committee (IPC). Taekwondo is a combat sport that combines ancient Asian heritage with modern values. It is a sport that is inclusive and accessible to everyone, regardless of age, gender, religion, ethnicity, or ability. The values of Taekwondo are based on the search for pleasure, self-improvement, perseverance, moral and physical strength, and respect for others.

- Vision: Taekwondo For All.
- Mission: The mission of WT is to develop and grow Taekwondo at all levels, from grassroots to elite, so that everyone has the opportunity to play, watch, and enjoy the sport.
- Values: The values of WT are inclusiveness, leadership, respect, tolerance, excellence, and integrity.
- Objectives: WT is responsible for the development, growth, and administration of Taekwondo worldwide. For the 2017-2021 cycle, WT has identified three strategic priorities:

1. Add value to the Olympic Movement: WT aims to contribute to the growth and success of the Olympic Movement by aligning its policies and practices with those of the IOC. WT seeks to champion Olympic values such as education, inclusiveness, friendship, solidarity, and fair play. WT also works closely with the Taekwondo Humanitarian Foundation for the development of sport.
2. Development of events: WT collaborates with organizing committees to ensure cost-efficient, sustainable events that leave a lasting legacy for local Taekwondo and sporting communities. WT seeks to ensure a coordinated and well-balanced event calendar that allows for participation at all levels and across all regions of the world. These high-quality events should promote the sport and athletes to new audiences.
3. The Development of Member Associations: The development of member associations is crucial for the success of World Taekwondo (WT). To achieve stronger events and greater grassroots growth, WT aims to enhance its support and training for key stakeholders. This includes sharing best practices in areas such as organization, administration, event management, good governance, gender equality, Olympic values, and sustainable development. To monitor and support the development of its members at all levels, WT uses various tools such as Global Membership Systems, MNA Survey, and Development Program. These tools help in areas such as administration, competition officials, coaches, entourage, athletes, and post-athletic career development. Important facts about WT: -

- Established on May 28, 1973.
- 213 member national associations.
- President is Dr. Chungwon Choue.
- Affiliated with SportAccord (GAISF) on October 8, 1975.
- Recognized by the IOC on July 17, 1980 (83rd IOC Session in Moscow).

- Affiliated with ASOIF on February 15, 1995.
- Demonstration sport at the 1988 Seoul Olympic Games and 1992 Barcelona Olympic Games.
- Official Olympic sport at the Sydney 2000 Olympic Games, recognized on September 4, 1994 (103rd IOC Session in Paris).
- Confirmed as one of the 25 core sports for the 2020 Tokyo Olympic Games by the IOC at its 125th Session in Buenos Aires on September 7-10, 2013.
- Taekwondo was included in the sports programs of the 2020 Tokyo Paralympics, including Para Taekwondo, at the 69th IPC Governing Board meeting held in Abu Dhabi, UAE from January 30 to February 1, 2015.
- Granted full membership by the IPC General Assembly in Mexico City, Mexico on November 15, 2015.
- Confirmed as one of the core sports programs of the 2024 Olympic Games in Paris by the IOC Session on September 18, 2017.
- Para Taekwondo was confirmed as part of the Paris 2024 Paralympic Games sports program by the IPC Governing Board on January 28, 2019.
- Virtual Taekwondo was announced as one of nine featured games at the Olympic Esports Series 2023 by the IOC on March 1, 2023.
- Member National Associations (MNAs):

(1) Asian Taekwondo Union-44 Members
(2) African Taekwondo Union-53 Members
(3) European Taekwondo Union-52 Members
(4) Oceanian Taekwondo Union-19 Members
(5) Pan America Taekwondo Union-45 Members

Organization

My Notes

Chapter 4

FEATURES AND PHILOSOPHY OF TAEKWONDO

FEATURES OF TAEKWONDO

Taekwondo is a martial art that emphasizes head-height, jumping, spinning, and fast kicking techniques. In fact, World Taekwondo (WT) competitions award extra points for strikes that include spinning kicks, kicks to the head, or both. The emphasis on speed and agility is one of the defining characteristics of taekwondo. This emphasis stems from Choi Hong-hi's analysis of biomechanics and Newtonian physics as the founder of taekwondo. Choi's Theory of Power, which he discovered, is still used in taekwondo training today. Choi's Theory of Power is based on the idea that the kinetic energy of a strike increases quadratically with strike speed but only linearly with strike mass. When it comes to generating power, speed is more important than size. He also promoted the "relax/strike" principle, which entails relaxing the body between blocks, kicks, and strikes and tensing the muscles only during the technique. This allows the practitioner to conserve energy while increasing the technique's power. Choi also introduced the "sine wave" technique, which involves raising one's center of gravity between techniques and lowering it as the technique is performed, resulting in the technique's characteristic up-and-down movement. Reaction force, concentration, equilibrium, breath control, and mass are all components of the Theory of Power. In order to provide more power to the striking limb, the reaction force principle involves bringing other parts of the body backward as the striking limb is brought forward. The principle of concentration is to bring as many muscles as possible to bear on a strike, concentrating the area of impact into as small an area as possible. Maintaining the correct center-of-balance throughout a technique is what equilibrium entails. Breath control advocates exhaling during a strike and ending the exhalation at the moment of impact. Finally, the mass principle emphasizes using as much of the body as possible to strike, such as rotating the hip along with the leg during a turning kick.

As previously stated, speed of execution of a technique is considered even more important than mass when it comes to providing power in taekwondo. Organizations such as the ITF and Kukkiwon define the general style of taekwondo, but individual clubs and schools tailor their practices. Although each taekwondo club or school is unique, a typical student will participate in most or all of the following activities:

1. Forms (pumsae or poomsae): A Form, also known as a Poomsae, is a choreographed pattern of defensive and offensive motions.
2. Sparring (Gyeorugi or Kyorugi): Sparring has several variations, including freestyle sparring (in which competitors fight for several minutes continuously), seven-, three-, two-, and one-step sparring (in which students practice pre-arranged sparring combinations), and point sparring (in which sparring is interrupted and then resumed after each point is scored.)
3. Breaking: Taekwondo uses a variety of techniques for testing, training, and martial arts demonstrations. Breaking boards, bricks, tiles, and ice or other material blocks are examples. Power breaking, speed

breaking, and special techniques that use jumping or flying techniques to achieve greater height, distance, or to clear obstacles are the three types of board breaking techniques.

Taekwondo also teaches self-defense, fundamental techniques like kicks, blocks, punches, and strikes, and throwing or falling techniques. Taekwondo practices include anaerobic and aerobic workouts, stretching, relaxation, and meditation exercises, as well as breathing control.

Taekwondo places a premium on mental and ethical discipline, etiquette, justice, respect, and self-confidence. The emphasis is not only on physical strength, but also on personal development and leadership abilities. Exams are given to students to assess their progress, and they are promoted to the next rank based on their performance.

Though most Taekwondo federation curricula do not include formal weapons training, individual schools may include additional training with weapons such as knives, swords, and sticks.

PHILOSOPHY OF TAEKWONDO

Taekwondo styles differ in their philosophical foundations. Many of these underpinnings, however, are historical references to the Hwarang's Five Commandments. Choi Hong-hi, for example, referred to the Five Tenets of Taekwondo as his philosophical foundation for taekwondo:

(1) Courtesy (yeui)
(2) Integrity (yeomchi)
(3) Perseverance (innae)
(4) Self-control (geukgi)
(5) Indomitable spirit (baekjeolbulgul)

These principles are further articulated in Choi's taekwondo oath:

I will follow the tenets of taekwondo.

I will show respect to the instructor and seniors.

I will never misuse taekwondo.

I will be a champion of liberty and justice.

I intend to create a more peaceful world.

Modern ITF organizations have updated and expanded on this philosophy.

The World Taekwondo (WT) also refers to the Hwarang commandments when articulating its taekwondo philosophy. It emphasizes the development of a peaceful society as one of the overarching goals of taekwondo practice, as does the ITF philosophy. This goal can be furthered, according to the WT's stated philosophy, by adopting the Hwarang spirit, behaving rationally, and acknowledging the philosophies embodied in the taegeuk (the yin and yang, i.e., "the unity of opposites") and the sam taegeuk (understanding change in the world as the interactions of the heavens, the Earth, and Man). The philosophical position of the Kukkiwon is also based on the Hwarang tradition.

My Notes

Chapter 5

BASIC TAEKWONDO VOCABULARY

Counting 1-100 (Native Korean)

1 -Hanah

2 -Dool

3 -Set

4 -Net

5 -Dasut

6 -Yosut

7 -Ill Gop

8 -Yo Dol

9 -A-Hoop

10 -Yoal

11 -Yoal-Hana…Etc

20-Soo Mool

21 -Soo Mool Hana...Etc

30 -Saroon

40 -Mahoon

50 -Shioon

60 –Yesoon

70 -Ilheun

80 -Yudoon

90 -Aheun

100 -Bak

Listings 1st-50th (Sino-Korean)

1st -Ill

2nd -Ee

3rd -Sam

4th -Sah

5th -Oh

6th -Yook

7th -Chil

8th -Pal

9th -Koo

10th -Ship

20th -Eeship

30th -Samship

40th -Sahship

50th -Ohship

Basic Terms

Training Area -Do Jang

Uniform -Do Boak or Dobok

Belt -Dhee

Grade, Rank or Color Belt -Geup

Degree (Black Belt) -Dan

Bow -KyungNeh

Yell -Keup

Form -Poomsae

Red -Hong

Blue -Chung

Sparring -Gyoroogi/Kyorugi

Breaking -Kyopka

Student -Hak Saeng, Koo Ga

Senior Student -Sun Bae Nim

Assistant Instructor (1 Dan) Chokyo Nim

Head of organization or GrandMaster -Kwan Jang Nim

Bow to Master -Kyung Neh

Hello -Annyong Hashimnigga

Goodbye -Annyonghi Kyeseyo

Please -Put'ak Hamnida

Thank you -Kamsa Hamnida

You are Welcome -Ch'un Man E Yo

Congratulations -Ch'ook Ha

Directions

Front -Up (Ap)

Back -Dwi

Side -Yop

High -Eulgool

Middle -Momtong

Low -Arae

Left -Wen

Right -Oreum

Outward -Bakkat

Inward -An

Downward -Naeryo

Upward -Allyo

Sideways (Turning) -Dollyo

Stances- Seogi or Sogi

Ready Stance -Cha Ryot Seogi

Ready Motion -Joonbe Seogi

Parallel Stance -Naranhi Seogi

Front Stance -Ap Koo Bi Seogi

Walking Stance -Ap Seogi

Back Stance -Dwitkoobi Seogi

Horse Ridding Stance -Joochoom Seogi

Cross Stance (Front) -Up-kkoa Seogi

Cross Stance (Back) -Dwi-kkoa Seogi

Crane Stance -Hakdari Seogi

Lef-hand Stance -Wen Seogi

Right-hand Stance -Oreum Seogi

Tiger Stance -Beom Seogi

Blocks- Makki

Down/Low Block - Arae Makki

High Block - Eulgool Makki

Inward Block - An Makki

Knife Hand Block (Double) - Sonnal Makki

Knife Hand Block (Single) - Han-Sonnal Makki

Middle Block - Momtong Makki

Outward Block - Bakkat Makki

Palm Hell Block - Batangson Makki

Scissors Block - Kawi Makki

Twist Block - Bituro Makki

Wide Open Block - Santeul Makki

Spreading Block - Hechyo Makki

X-Block - Otgoreo Makki

Strike

Strike -Chigi

Knife-hand Strike (Inward) -Sonnal An-Chigi

Knife-hand Strike (Outward) -Sonnal Bakkat-Chigi

Hammer Fist (Down) -Meori-Naeryo Chigi

Palm Heel Strike -Batangson Teok-Chigi

Elbow Strike -Palkup Chigi

Knee Strike -Mureup Chigi

Back Fist Strike -Deung Jumeok Chigi

Fingertips Thrust -Kawinsonkkeut Tzireuki

Punch

Punch -Jireuki

Reverse Punch -Bahro Jireuki

Straight Punch -Bandae Jireuki

Middle Punch -Momtong Jireuki

Upper Cut Punch -Chi Jireuki

Side Punch -Yop Jireuki

Hook Punch -Dollyo Jireuki

Downward Punch -Naeryo Jireuki

Erected Fist Punch -Sewo Jireuki

Basic Kicks

Front Kick -Ap Chagi

Roundhouse Kick -Ap Dollyo Chagi

Side Kick -Yop Chagi

Half Moon kick -Badal Chagi

Axe kick -Nareyo or Chiko Chagi

High Stretch Kick (straight leg) -Ap-Olligi or Krohlligi

Back Kick -Dwi Chagi

Hook Kick -Nakka Chagi

Thrashing or Spinning Kick -Huryo Chagi

Push Kick -Mireo Chagi

Stretch kick -Ap-Ollyo Chagi

Swing Kick (Outward) -Bakkat Chagi

Swing Kick (Inward) -An Chagi

Target Kick -Pyojeok Chagi

Twist Kick -Bitureo Chagi

Anatomical Terms

Foot -Bal

Palm -Batang Son

Leg -Dari

Heel Back -Dwikoomchi

Heel Bottom -Dwichook

Fist -Joomeok

Neck -Mok

Body -Mom

Knee -Mooreup

Arm -Pal

Elbow -Palkoop

Forearm -Palmok

Hand -Son

Wrist -Sonmoke

Knife Hand -Sonnal

Chin -Teok

My Notes

Chapter 6

POOMSAE

Poomsae is a Korean word that means 'patterns' or 'forms'. It is a predetermined sequence of defense and offense movements used in Taekwondo for fundamental training and skill practice. Poomsae practice includes almost all Taekwondo techniques, and all steps should be performed as if facing an attacker. Poomsae is also used to take the next rank (belt) exam all the way up to the Black Belt. Up to the Black Belt, there are eight Poomsae forms called 'Taegeuk'. Taegeuk is the 'Universe' from which all elements and objects are created. It is also the central symbol of South Korea's flag. Taegeuk is derived from Taegeukgi (Hangul, gi: Flag) and is commonly associated with 'Korean Taoism philosophy' and 'Korean Shamanism'. The Korea Taekwondo Association appointed a committee of representatives from six of the Nine Kwans in 1965 to develop the forms for what is now known as Kukkiwon- or WT-style taekwondo. The committee introduced the 'Palgwae' and 'Yudanja' (Black Belt) forms two years later, in 1967, which included a simplified version of Koryo. Two more kwans joined the committee in 1971. Taegeuk 1 to 3 are for basic blocks, punches, and kicks, while Taegeuk 4 and 5 are for intermediate grades. Taegeuk 6 and 7 are practiced at the advanced level, and Taegeuk 8 is required for the black belt grading exam. Taegeuk 1-8 are known as the following in Korean:

1. Taegeuk Il Jang
2. Taegeuk Ih Jang
3. Taegeuk Sam Jang
4. Taegeuk Sa Jang
5. Taegeuk Oh Jang
6. Taegeuk Yook Jang
7. Taegeuk Chil Jang
8. Taegeuk Pal Jang.

1. Taegeuk Il Jang
('The Sky' or 'The Heaven')

Here are some important points to remember about Taegeuk Il Jang, the first poomsae in Kuki-style Taekwondo 8th grade (Geup) students. This poomsae is practiced to advance to the next rank, which is 7th geup. The name Taegeuk Il Jang means "Part 1 of the Taegeuk". "Il" means 1 in the Sino-Korean numbering system, and "jang" means "chapter" or "part". The floor pattern of each taegeuk poomsae consists of three parallel lines, and a 180-degree turn is performed on each line. If the turn is made by pivoting in place, the line is considered to be broken. If the turn is made by moving the lead foot to the rear, the line is considered to be solid.

The floor pattern of each Taegeuk poomsae is composed of three broken or solid lines, known as trigrams or gwae, which correspond to natural elements. Taegeuk Il Jang, for instance, is associated with the trigram comprising three solid lines, representing "the sky" or "the heavens". In Daoist philosophy, the sky symbolizes creation or beginnings. Therefore, Taegeuk Il Jang is considered the "creation" of a new Taekwondo student, marking the student's new beginning. The movements in Taegeuk Il Jang are primarily upright, with an open body posture, similar to the sky.

The poomsae includes techniques such as walking stance, long front stance, low block, high block, inside middle block, middle punch, and front snap kick.

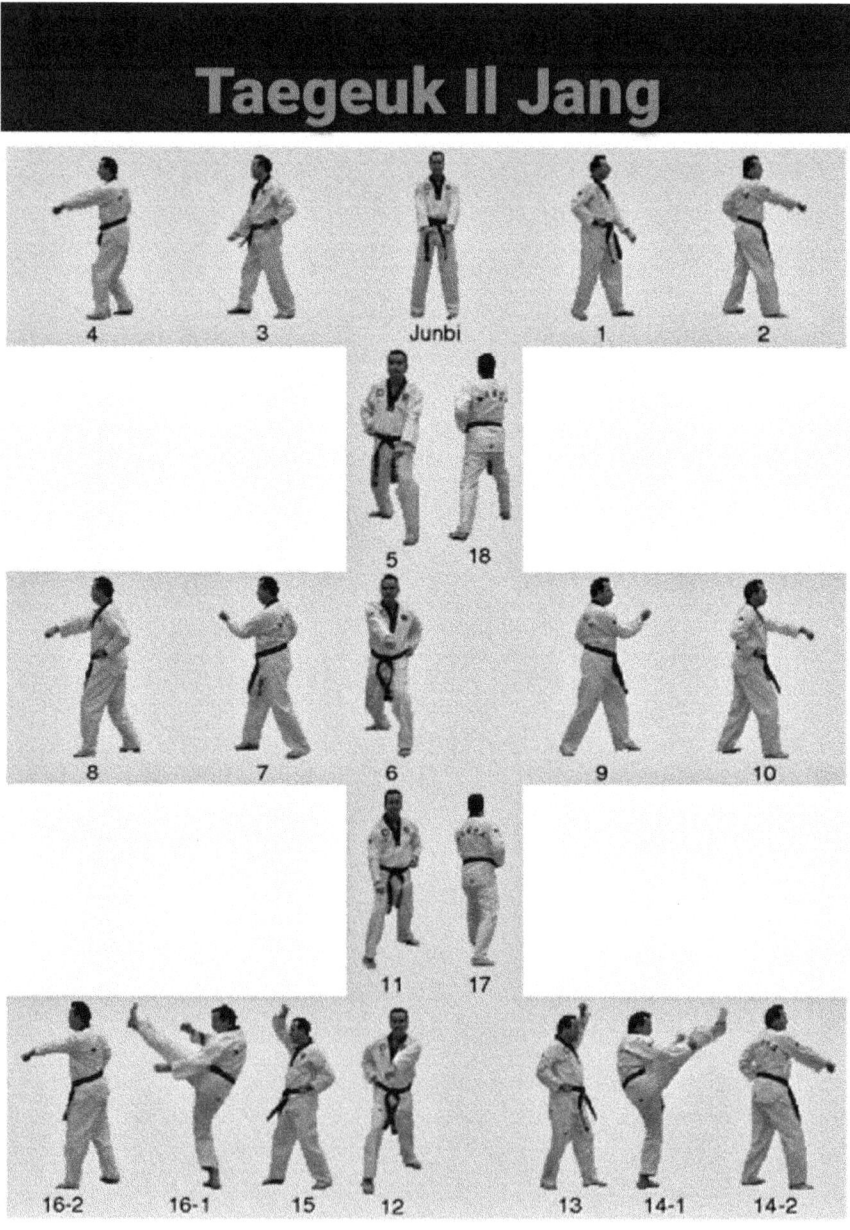

2. Taegeuk Ee Jang
(Lake)

In Kukkiwon/WT-style taekwondo, seventh group students practice Taegeuk Ee Jang to advance to the next rank (6th geup). This form means "Part 2 of the Taegeuk" and has two solid lines and one broken line, which represents "lake." The form starts with two turns performed by moving the lead foot and ends with a pivot in place. The Kukkiwon emphasizes that Taegeuk Ee Jang should be performed with a tranquil and clear mind, just like the calm waters of a lake.

The techniques involved in this form include a walking stance, long front stance, low block, inside middle block, high block, middle punch, and front snap kick. Additionally, Taegeuk Ee Jang introduces high punch, how to transition from a walking stance to a long front stance, and how to perform a kick-and-punch combination.

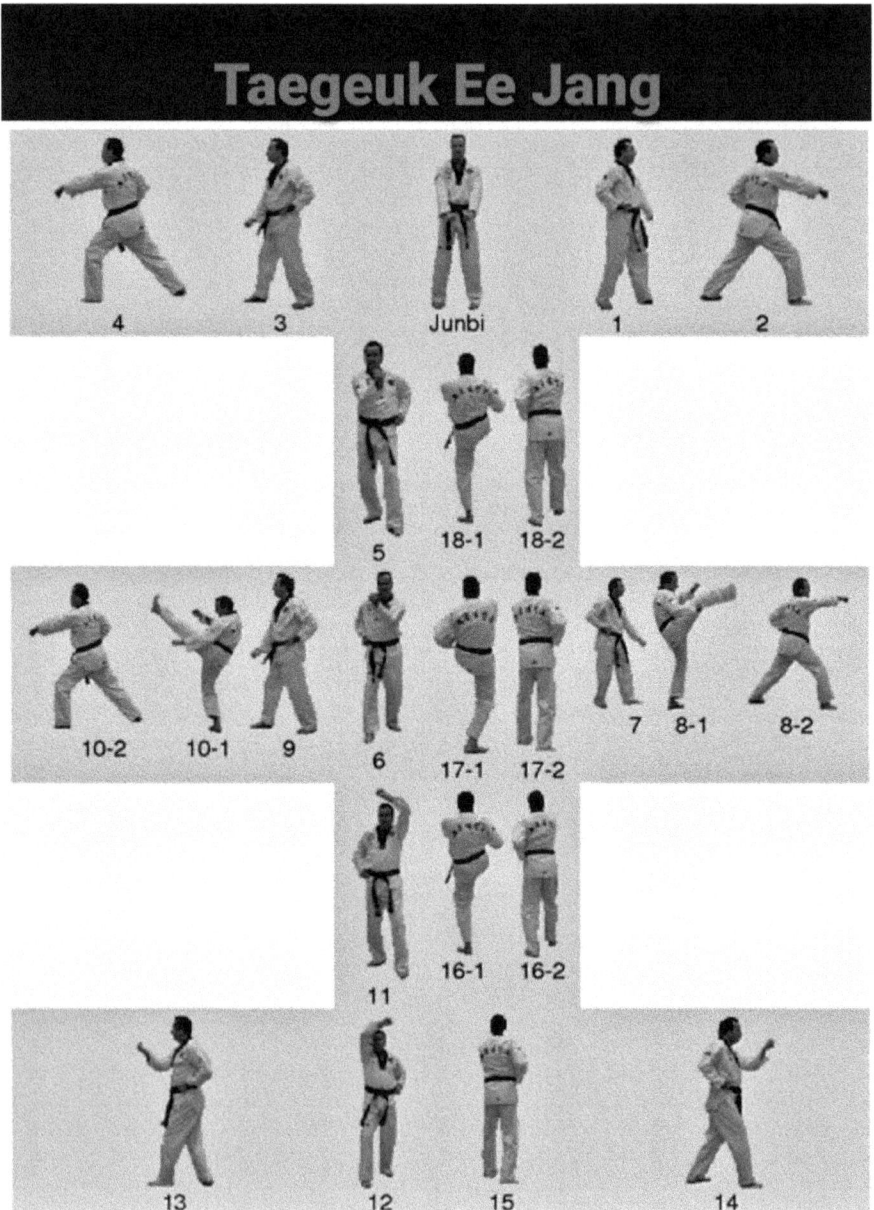

3. Taegeuk Sam Jang
(Fire)

In Kukkiwon/WT-style taekwondo, students of the sixth group practice a form called Taegeuk Sam Jang to advance to the next rank (5th geup). Taegeuk Sam Jang translates to "Part 3 of the Taegeuk". The form involves three turns, with the first and last turns performed by moving the lead foot and the middle turn performed by pivoting in place. This represents the trigram for fire ("yi"), which consists of a solid line, a broken line, and a solid line. The Kukkiwon emphasizes that Taegeuk Sam Jang should be performed with energy, like a fire.

The techniques involved in Taegeuk Sam Jang are: Knife-Hand Technique, Neck-high knife-hand strike, Knifehand outward block, Front kick followed by a double punch, and Low block, punch, kick combination.

Taegeuk Sam Jang

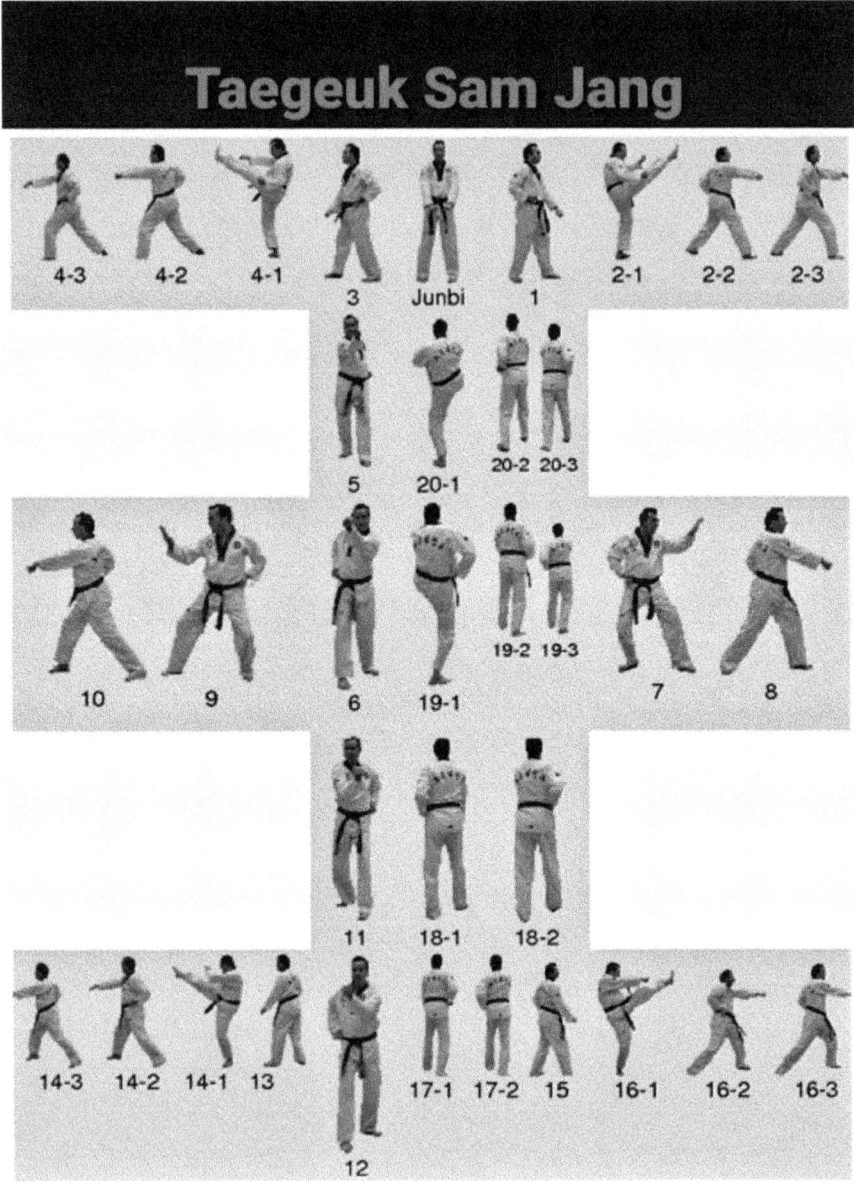

4. Taegeuk Sa Jang
(Thunder)

Fifth group students of Kukkiwon/WT-style taekwondo practice the Taegeuk Sa Jang form in order to advance to the next rank (4th geup). Its name translates to "Taegeuk Part 4." The first turn of the form is performed by moving the lead foot, whereas the final two turns necessitate the use of a pivot. This implies that the associated trigram is a solid line followed by two broken lines, which represents the thunder ("jin") trigram. The Taegeuk Sa Jang poomsae, according to the Kukkiwon, should be performed with majesty, much like a thunderstorm. It is the first poomsae in the Taegeuk series that allows a practitioner to transition directly from the first line to the third line through a continuous sequence of movements, further symbolizing a thunderstorm's long reach.

The Taegeuk Sa Jang form includes the following techniques: Double Knifehand Block or Augmented Outside Knifehand Block, which is a staple of subsequent Taegeuk poomsae, Spearhead Thrust, Side Kick, The Sallowform Strike, A Simultaneous Knifehand High Block, Knifehand Neck Strike, and Chambering for the next movement. In this context, "chamber" refers to being ready for an upcoming movement. For example, if the trainee is performing two side kicks, he must chamber for a Double Knifehand Block while still performing the kick.

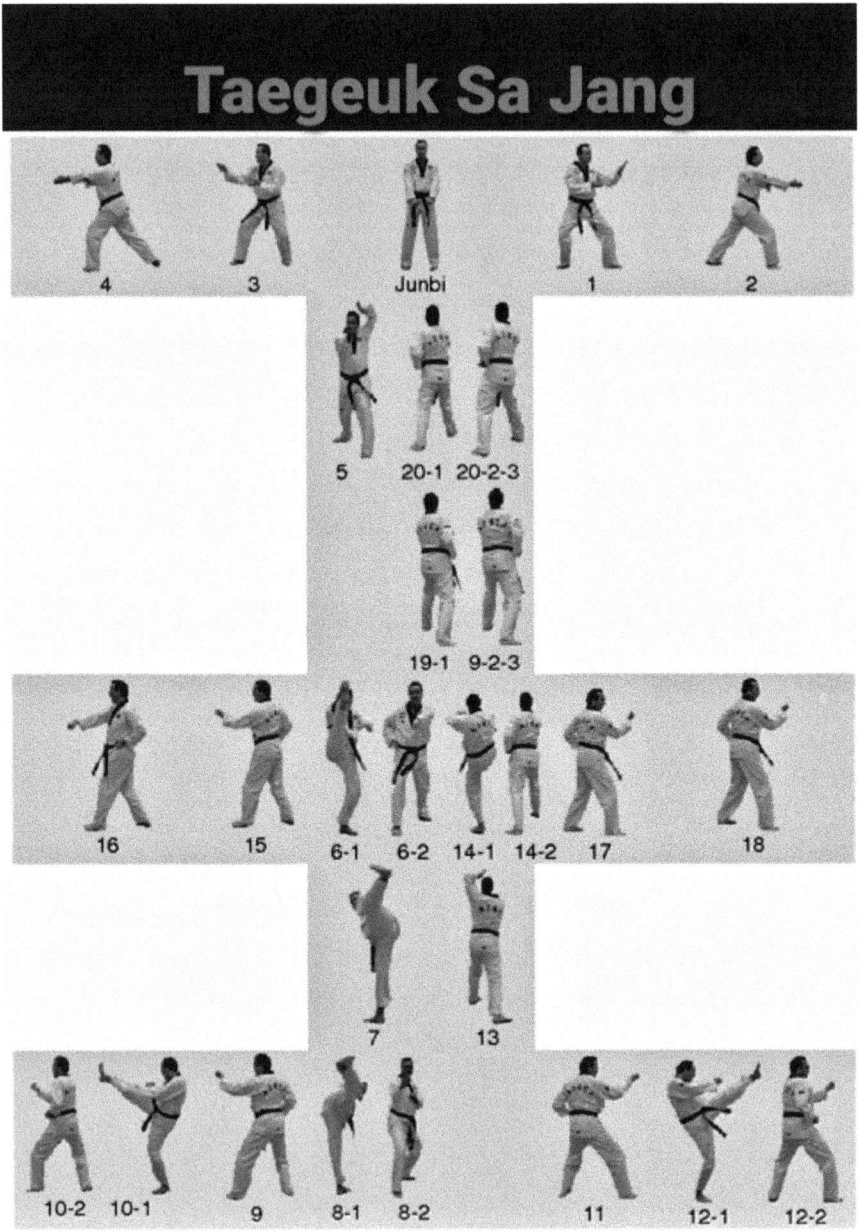

5. Taegeuk Oh Jang
(Wind)

Taegeuk Oh Jang is a form used by the fourth group of Kukkiwon/WT-style taekwondo students to advance to the next rank (3rd geup). Its name translates to "Taegeuk Part 5." The practitioner pivots in place during the first turn of Taegeuk Oh Jang, while they move their lead foot during the final two turns. This form's associated trigram is a broken line, a solid line, and another solid line, representing the trigram for 'wind' ("seon"). The Kukkiwon emphasizes that this poomsae should be performed with gentle but unyielding movements, similar to the wind.

Taegeuk Oh Jang's techniques include various types of elbow strikes introduced in the form. Along the top line, a helping hand supports chin-height elbow strikes, while the off-hand serves as a target for solar-plexus-height elbow strikes. Side kicks along the middle line are also combined with a simultaneous hand strike.

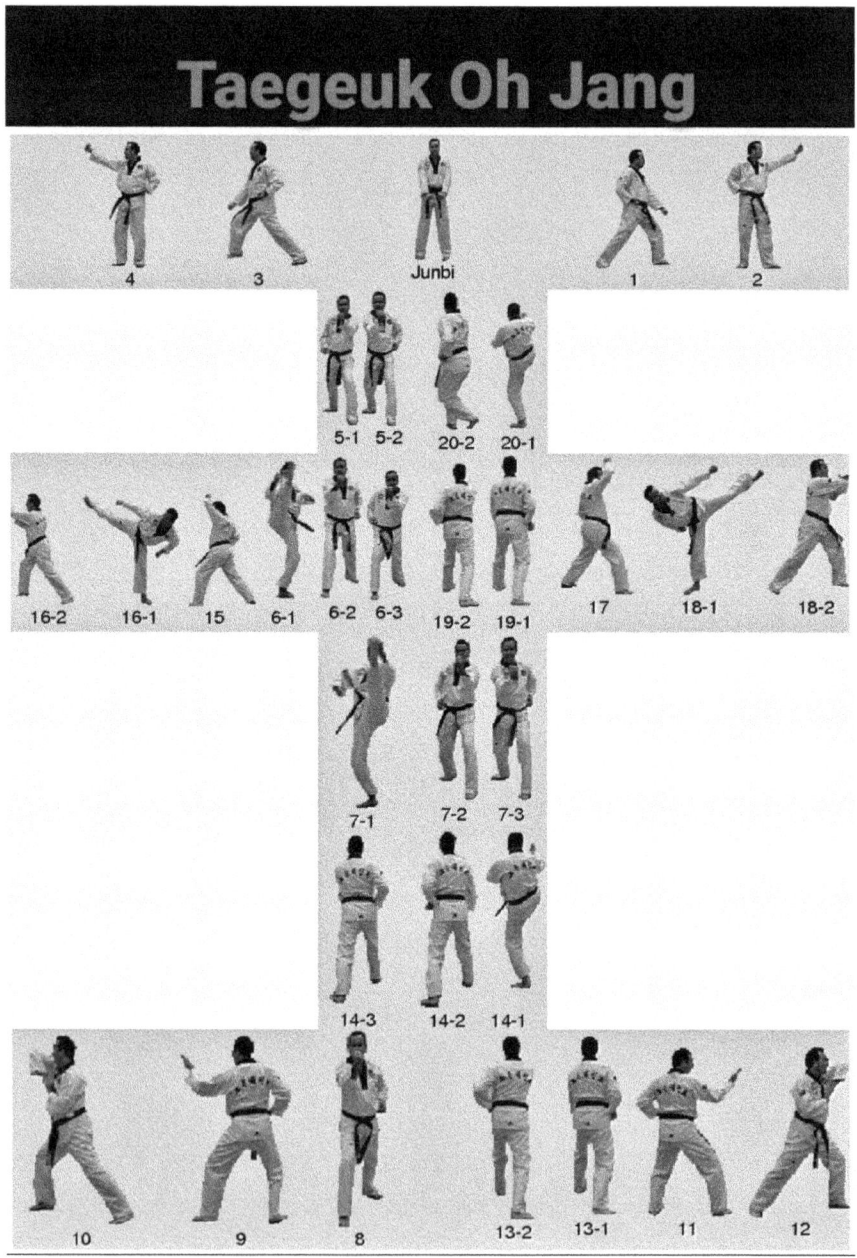

6. Taegeuk Yook Jang
(Water)

In Kukkiwon/WT-style taekwondo, third-group students practice Taegeuk Yook Jang to advance to the next rank (2nd geup). The form is also known as "Part 6 of the Taegeuk". To perform the form correctly, the first turn of Taegeuk Sa Jang requires a pivot in place, while the second turn involves moving the lead foot. The final turn is then performed by pivoting in place. This sequence of movements symbolizes the trigram for water ("gam"), which is represented by a broken line, a solid line, and a broken line. The Kukkiwon emphasizes the importance of performing Taegeuk Yook Jang with fluid movements that imitate the flow of water around an opponent. This poomsae aims to wear down the opponent in a similar way, making the techniques smooth and circular.

The form includes several techniques such as a Twist Block followed by a roundhouse kick, which creates a circular movement between lines. The Palm Blocks and the rearward steps into the back stance and front stance are also featured. This is the only poomsae with rearward stepping motions. Additionally, the Slow Low Opening Block at the Centre is performed to an 8-count.

7. Taegeuk Chil Jang
(Mountain)

The Taegeuk Chil Jang form is practiced by second group students of Kukkiwon/WT-style taekwondo to advance to the next rank (1st geup). Its name translates to "Part 7 of the Taegeuk". The first two turns of the form are performed by pivoting in place, while the final turn is executed by moving the lead foot. The associated trigram for this form is a broken line, a broken line, and a solid line, representing the mountain ("gan"). The Kukkiwon emphasizes that the movements in this poomsae should be unyielding and immovable, like a mountain.

In terms of techniques, the Taegeuk Chil Jang form includes: Tiger Stance, as tigers are associated with life in mountains in Korean culture, Low Double Knifehand Block (also known as Low Augmented Knifehand Block), A Palm Block and a Backfist Strike, A Scissors Block (which involves a simultaneous Low Block and Outside Block), A Shoulder Height Opening Block, A Knee Strike to the abdomen, A Target Kick, and A Hinge-Block chamber leading up to a Low Cross Block. This is the first block that is not a deflecting block and traps an attack rather than deflecting it, demonstrating the "immovable" and "unyielding" movements emphasized in this form.

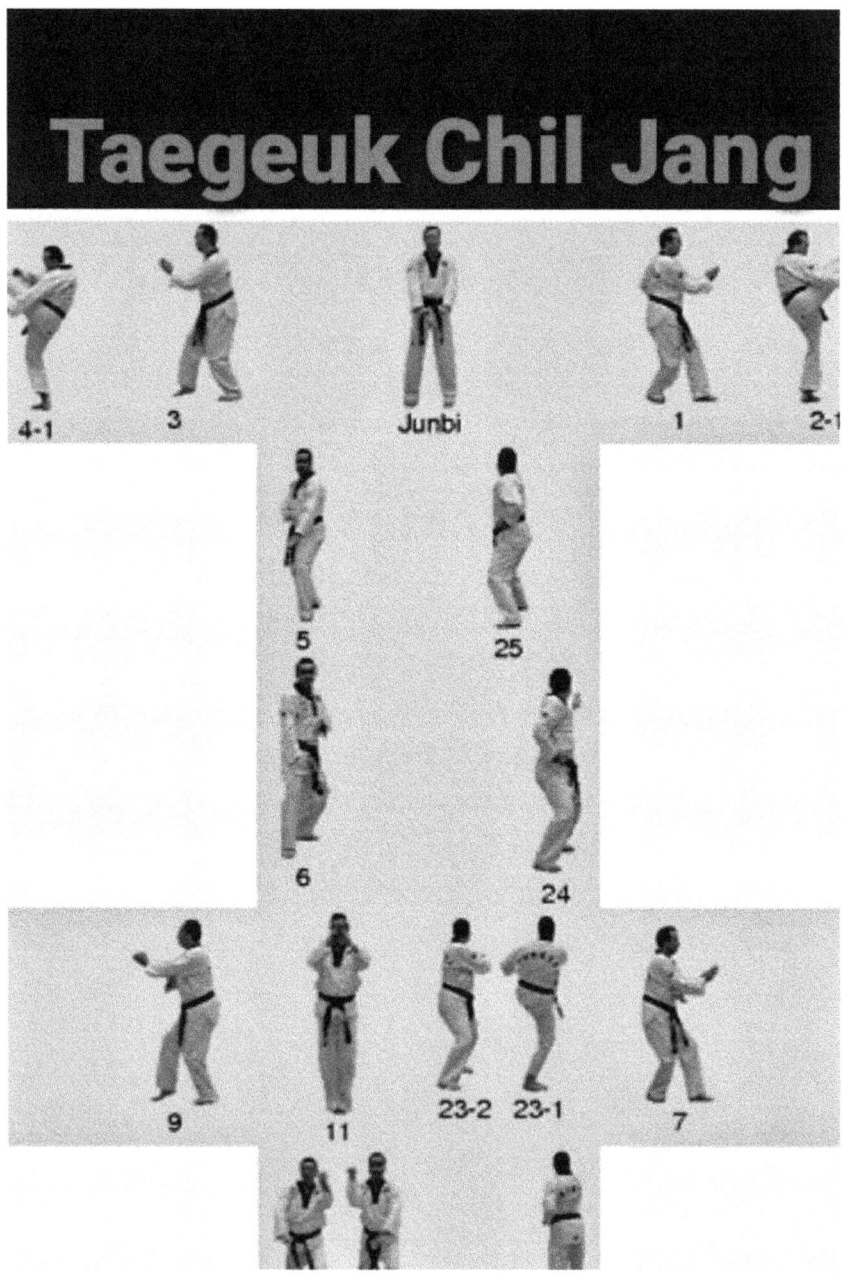

8. Taegeuk Pal Jang
(Earth)

The Taegeuk Pal Jang form is practiced by first geup students of Kukkiwon/WT-style taekwondo to advance to the next rank, usually the 1st dan black belt. At this point, students begin to study a new sequence of black belt forms. Taegeuk Pal Jang is translated as "Part 8 of the Taegeuk." All three turns in the Taegeuk Pal Jang form involve pivoting in place, with the turn on the third line considered a pivot-in-place since it uses a cross stance as a transitional movement. This indicates that the associated trigram for this form is three broken lines, which represents the trigram for earth ("gon"). According to the Kukkiwon, this poomsae serves as the foundation (i.e., the earth) for the student's future training (i.e., black belt training).

The techniques involved in Taegeuk Pal Jang include consolidating prior lessons, augmented outside blocks (medium and low heights), cross stance (used as a transitional movement on the third line), half mountain block, forward-facing double knifehand block, a single upward jump in which the practitioner kicks twice (once with each leg) while still in the air, and one front kick performed on the ground, followed immediately by a single jump front kick.

Taegeuk Pal Jang

My Notes

Chapter 7

KYORUGI

Aim and Purpose of Kyorugi

- Kyorugi's Aim and Purpose

Kyorugi serves a variety of functions that benefit both physical and mental health. The following are six reasons why people participate in Kyorugi:

1. Physical fitness and conditioning - Kyorugi is a great form of cardiovascular exercise that helps people improve their strength, flexibility, overall fitness, and endurance. Regular Kyorugi training improves agility, coordination, and speed.
2. Mental discipline and focus - Kyorugi necessitates mental discipline and focus. To effectively anticipate and react to their opponent's moves, participants must sharpen their concentration, strategic thinking, and awareness during combat. This aspect fosters discipline, resilience, and the ability to remain calm in stressful situations.
3. Skill Development - Kyorugi allows students to hone their striking and blocking techniques, combinations, footwork, and timing. Practicing these techniques improves overall skill proficiency and reinforces muscle memory.
4. Self Defense- Kyorugi is a martial art that provides its practitioners with a number of advantages. For starters, it teaches them the

necessary skills and techniques for defending themselves in real-life situations. Practitioners learn to react quickly, assess their opponent's movements, and execute appropriate defensive strategies by engaging in controlled combat scenarios.
5. Competition and Achievements- Kyorugi offers participants the opportunity to compete at various levels, from local tournaments to national and international competitions. Students can set goals, track their progress, and challenge themselves to improve through competition. Kyorugi success can lead to a sense of accomplishment and self-confidence.
6. Sportsmanship and Respect- Kyorugi emphasizes sportsmanship and respect for one's opponent. Participants learn to compete with integrity, adhering to established rules and regulations while treating their sparring partner with respect and courtesy. This encourages character development, moral values, and ethical behavior.

Competition Area

The competition area must have a flat surface and be free of any obstacles that could injure the competitors. It should be covered with a non-slippery, elastic mat. It can be installed on a platform that is 0.6-1m high from the ground if necessary. The outer boundary line must be inclined at a gradient of less than 30 degrees for safety reasons. The competition area can be divided into two shapes:

1. Square Shape: The contest area should be 8m x 8m in size and surrounded by a safety zone that is roughly equidistant on all sides. The competition area should be no smaller than 10m x 10m and no larger than 12m x 12m, including the contest area and the safety area. If the competition area is on a platform, the safety area can be expanded as needed to ensure contestant's safety. As specified in the relevant competition operational manual, the contest area and the safety area should be of different colors.

2. Octagonal Shape: The competition area should be square, measuring no less than 10m x 10m and no more than 12m x 12m. The octagonal-shaped contest area should be located in the center of the competition area. The contest area should be approximately 8m in diameter, with each side of the octagon measuring approximately 3.3m in length. The safety area should be located between the outer line of the competition area and the contest area's boundary line. As specified in the relevant competition operational manual, the contest area and the safety area should be of different colors.

Contestant

A contestant must meet certain qualifications, according to the rules. The following are the qualifications:

1) The contestant must be a member of the participating team's nationality.
2) The WT MNA (Member National Association) must recommend him/her.
3) The contestant must have a Kukkiwon or WT Taekwondo Dan/Poom Certificate.
4) He or she must be in possession of a WT Global Athlete License (GAL).
5) For senior tournaments, the contestant must be at least 17 years old, 15-17 years old for junior championships, and 12-14 years old for cadet championships. However, the age criteria for Youth Olympic Games may differ depending on the IOC's decision.
6. A WT-approved dobok or competition uniform, trunk PSS (Protector and Scoring System), head PSS, groin guard, forearm guards, shin guards, gloves, and sensing socks (if using PSS) are required. Before entering the field of play, he or she must have a mouthpiece and a head protector firmly tucked under their left arm. Before the start of the

competition, they must put on the head protector as instructed by the referee.
7. Furthermore, at WT-sponsored or recognized Taekwondo events, the use or administration of drugs or chemical substances on the WADA prohibited list is strictly prohibited. The WADA anti-doping code shall apply to Taekwondo competitions at the Olympic Games and other multi-sport games, while the WT anti-doping rules shall apply to WT promoted and/or recognized championships.

Contest Duration

The competition will be divided into three rounds of two minutes each, with a one-minute break in between. If the scores are tied at the end of the third round, a one-minute golden round will be held following a one-minute break. The length of each round can be adjusted to suit specific championships, with options ranging from 1 minute for 3 rounds, 1 minute 30 seconds for 3 rounds, 2 minutes for 2 rounds, or 5 minutes for 1 round, with each contestant allowed one 30-second time-out. The final decision on the duration of each round for the relevant championships will be made by the Technical Delegate.

Contest Procedure

1. Organize a contest.
2. Examine the body, uniform, and apparatus.
3. Getting into the competition zone.
4. The referee will begin the competition by saying "Joon-bi" (ready) and "Shi-jak" (start).
5. The referee shall declare "Shi-jak" at the start of each round of competition.
6. The referee shall declare "Keu-man" (stop) at the end of each round of competition. If the referee does not declare "Keu-man," the contest is declared over when the match clock runs out. However, "Gam-jeom"

can be given and recorded in the score even after the match clock has expired.
7. The referee may pause a contest by saying "Kal-yeo" (pause) and resume it by saying "Kye-sok" (continue). The recorder should immediately stop the match time when the referee declares "Kal-yeo." The recorder should immediately restart the match time when the referee declares "Kye-sok."
8. At the conclusion of the final round, the referee declares the winner by raising their hand to the winner's side.

Contest Procedure in Team Competition: -

1. Both teams must line up in the submitted team order, facing each other, towards the first boundary line from the contestant's marks.
2. The procedure before and after the contest shall be carried out in accordance with clause 4 and 6 of this article.
3. Both teams must exit the competition area and wait in the designated area for each contestant's match.
4. Immediately following the conclusion of the final match, both teams must line up in the contest area facing each other.
5. The referee declares the winning team by raising their own hand to the side of the winning team.

Allowed Techniques and Areas

The following are the permitted fighting techniques and areas: -

Techniques that are permitted:

1. Fist Technique - A straight punch delivered with the knuckle of a tightly clenched fist.
2. Foot Technique - Any technique that uses any part of the foot below the ankle bone.

Permitted Areas:

1. Trunk - On the areas covered by the trunk protector, you can use fist and foot techniques. However, you are not permitted to attack the spine.
2. Head - Only foot techniques are permitted above the collarbone.

Points to Consider

In a Taekwondo match, the following valid points can be scored:

- Scoring Zones:

1. Trunk: The trunk protector's blue or red colored area.
2. Head: The entire upper portion of the head above the bottom line of the head protector.

- Valid Points Criteria:

1. Points will be awarded when a permitted technique is delivered with the appropriate level of impact to the scoring areas of the trunk.
2. When a permitted technique is delivered to the scoring areas of the head, a point(s) will be awarded.
3. Except fist techniques, the electronic scoring system will determine the validity of the technique, level of impact, and/or valid contact to the scoring area. These decisions will not be subject to immediate video replay.
4. The WT technical committee will determine the required level of impact and sensitivity of the scoring system using different scales, taking into account weight category, gender, and age groups. The Technical Delegate may recalibrate the valid level of impact in certain circumstances.

- Points to Consider:

1. A valid punch to the trunk protector earns one (1) point.
2. Two (2) points for a valid trunk protector kick.
3. Four (4) points for a valid trunk protector turning kick.
4. Three (3) points for a valid head kick.
5. Five (5) points for a valid turning kick to the head.
6. Each "Gam-Jeom" given to the opposing contestant will earn one (1) point.

- The match score will be the total of the three rounds' points.
- If a prohibited act or move is followed by a point(s), the referee will declare a penalty for the prohibited act and the point(s) will be null and void.

Penalties and Prohibited Acts

Taekwondo's prohibited acts and penalties are designed with the following goals in mind:

1. To ensure the contestant's safety.
2. To ensure fair competition.
3. Encourage the application of appropriate techniques.

- The penalty is declared by the referee, and prohibited acts are penalized with "Gam-jeom" (Deduction Penalty).
- One "Gam-jeom" equals one point for the opposing contestant.
- Taekwondo prohibits the following behaviors:
  1. Crossing the dividing line.
  2. Tumbling down.
  3. Avoiding or postponing the game.
  4. Snatching or pushing the opponent.

5. Lifting a leg or kicking in the air for more than 3 seconds to obstruct the opponent's potential attacking movements or kick aimed below the waist.
6. Kicking beneath the waist.
7. Attacking the opponent following "Kal-yeo"
8. Using the hand to strike the opponent's head.
9. Knee-butting or knee-attacking.
10. Attacking the downed opponent.
11. Attacking trunk PSS with the side or bottom of the foot in a clinch position with the knee pointed out.
12. Misconduct of a competitor or coach, which includes:

(a) failing to comply with a referee's command or decision.
(b) Protesting the official's decision in an inappropriate manner.
(c) Unacceptable attempts to disrupt or influence the outcome of the game.
(d) Intimidating or insulting the opposing competitor or coach.
(e) Unaccredited team doctors, physiotherapists, athlete trainers, or chiropractors, as well as other team officials, who are discovered seated in the doctor's position.
(f) Any other serious misconduct or unsportsmanlike behavior by a competitor or coach.

13. If a coach or competitor engages in excessive misconduct and fails to obey the referee's instructions, the referee may declare a sanction request by raising a yellow card. In this case, the competition supervisory board must investigate the behavior of the contestant and/or coach and decide whether a sanction is appropriate.
14. If a contestant refuses to comply with the competition rules or the referee's orders on purpose and repeatedly, the referee may end the match by raising a yellow card and declaring the opposing contestant the winner.

15. If the referee at the inspection desk or officials on the field of play determine, in consultation with the PSS technician if necessary, that a contestant or coach attempted to manipulate the sensitivity of the PSS sensor(s) and/or inappropriately altered the PSS so as to affect its performance, the contestant is disqualified.
16. When a contestant receives ten (10) "Gam-jeom," the referee must declare the contestant a loser via a punitive declaration (PUN).
17. "Gam-Jeom" will be factored into the overall score of the three rounds.

Decisions

Here are the different ways a fighter can win a match:

1. RSC - Win by Referee Stops Contest
2. PTF - Win by Final Score
3. PTG - Win by Point Gap
4. GDP - Win by Golden Points
5. SUP - Win by Superiority
6. WDR - Win by Withdrawal
7. DSQ - Win by Disqualification
8. PUN - Win by Referees Punitive Declaration
9. DQB - Win by Disqualification for Unsportsmanlike Behaviour

Knock down

When a proper attack is delivered and one of the following occurs, a knockdown is declared:

1. Any part of the body other than the sole makes contact with the floor as a result of the force of the opponent's scoring technique.
2. As a result of the opponent's scoring techniques, a contestant is dazed and shows no intention or ability to continue.

3. The referee determines that the contest cannot be continued due to a valid scoring technique.

- The referee will declare "Kal-yeo" (Break) to keep the attacker away from the downed contestant. The "Kal-yeo" command will bring the match clock to a halt.
- The referee will first check the status of the downed contestant before counting aloud from "Hanah" (One) to "Yeol" (Ten) at one-second intervals, making hand signals to indicate the passage of time.
- If a downed contestant stands up during the referee's count and wishes to continue the fight, the referee will count up to "Yeo-dul" (Eight) for the contestant's recovery.
- The referee will then determine whether the contestant has recovered and, if so, will declare "Kye-sok" (Continue).
- If a knocked-down contestant cannot demonstrate the desire to resume the contest by the count of "Yeo-dul" (Eight), the referee will declare the other contestant the winner by RSC (Referee Stops Contest).

My Notes

Chapter 8

NEEL'S TAEKWONDO DIARY

Name-Neel

Std.-5th

Subject -Taekwondo

Day 1:

Today was my first day of Taekwondo class. I didn't want to join, but my mom forced me to. After getting tired from school, I used to be able to lie down and watch TV in the evening, but now that won't be possible. I'll do it for a few days and then try to persuade my mom by giving some good reasons. Mom left me in the class after chatting with coach Ram sir for a while. He chatted with me too and I realized he has a good nature. He told me to practice less today or my feet would be sore tomorrow, but I didn't listen and said that playing cricket every day would make this practice easy. He said it was okay and I did the whole practice and stretching. After the class, I came out of the hall (Sir called it 'Dojang') and chatted with Sir again. Mom was waiting near the gate. On the way,

I asked Sir how many people I could fight with at once after learning Taekwondo. Sir just smiled and left.

Day 2:

OMG... I could barely sit up this morning. My legs were very sore. Mummy held my hand and led me to the bathroom. Dad and Didi (my elder sister) were laughing at me. Mummy also started laughing with them. I was very angry with her because she was the one who forcefully sent me to Taekwondo class. Somehow the day passed and I was afraid to go to class in the evening but mommy is very strict so she took me. Sir and I went to the hall together. Sir smiled and asked if my feet hurt. I frantically tried to say no but he recognized it. He smiled and said to do as he says for now. No stretching today. My legs felt a little better after the class. Sir also gave me a Taekwondo uniform today, which was so cool! I took some pictures in my uniform and put them on my status. Everyone replied with compliments and it made me feel happy.

Day 3:

Not much leg pain today. Sir taught us white belt students some instructions such as Charyuht-Attention, Kyung neh-Bow, Joonbe-Ready.

Day 4:

Today, I tried kicking on the kicking pad but my finger hurt a lot. Since coming from the class, my toe has been very sore. Mom applied ointment to my finger and it feels a little better now.

Day 5:

Today, Coach Sir spent some time chatting with us, the white belt students, and explained a lot about Taekwondo. He told us that Taekwondo is a martial art from South Korea that uses the Korean language in its instructions. I now understand why the instructions are so difficult. I was wondering where Korea is located, as I've heard the name before but couldn't remember. The class is off tomorrow, and he asked everyone to practice at home. I'm looking forward to practicing tomorrow!

Day 6:

I didn't practice today.

Day 7:

Today, Coach Sir made me do some stretching and then practice kicking on the kickpad. However, I still can't kick properly, and my leg hurts. Sir advised that while performing the Dollyo Chagi (Turning Kick), the feet should slap on the kickpad to ensure the kick is correct and to avoid injury. I'm trying my best, but again my fingers hurt. Can I…?

Day 8:

"No pain, no gain!"

Day 9:

Today, I was finally able to hit a couple of good kicks on the kickpad without any pain. Coach Sir complimented me on my progress. Once I perfect my kick, I'll show it off to Yash and the rest of the class. I'll be a hero in front of everyone!

Day 10:

Abhishek, a senior black belt student in the class, advised me to bow to the dojang before entering the class and also to bow to master and seniors as a sign of respect. He also shared with me a great quote: "When you are learning about Taekwondo, it is about respect."

Day 11:

Today, the instructor started teaching the first Poomsae to the white belt students. He went over the instructions and demonstrated the first two steps. I didn't understand anything, and my head started spinning. I feel lost!

Day 12:

Today, most of my kicks hit well above the pad, and the coach taught us four more steps of Poomsae. I was able to do it immediately. It wasn't too difficult after all!

Day 13:

Today, the class was off, so I practiced at home for some time. I taught Didi some Poomsae steps and explained the instructions for Taekwondo to her. However, she didn't understand anything and even told me that I was talking stupid. She can't understand Korean, so it was hard to explain.

Day 14:

Tae means "foot", "leg", or "to step on"; Kwon means "fist" or "fight"; and Do means "way" or "discipline". The five tenets of Taekwondo are courtesy, integrity, perseverance, self-control, and indomitable spirit.

Day 15:

Today, Coach Sir made me do some stretching exercises and practiced kicks on the pad. I performed well. He encouraged us to continue practicing kicks and poomsae at home.

Day 16:

After coming back from class, I tried practice my kicks at home on a cement pillar. Unfortunately, I lost control and ended up hurting my leg. I cried for a long time and my mom applied an ointment to my leg. I might not be able to attend the class tomorrow. It reminded me of one of the five tenets of Taekwondo – Self Control.

Day 17:

Due to leg pain, I had to skip class today and even took leave from school. My mother received a call from my coach in the evening who said that my injury wasn't serious and that I should attend the class tomorrow.

Day 18:

When I arrived at the class today, my coach reminded us that taking a break for a small injury could impact our performance in matches and belt promotion tests. I was worried as I had promised my friends that I would get the yellow belt. I decided not to take a break from the class anymore.

Day 19:

Today, I watched Abhishek and Lucky, two senior students, play a Taekwondo match live for the first time. After the match, I asked my coach many questions and expressed my desire to play a match too. However, he said that I need more practice and equipment before I can participate in a match.

Day 20:

I practiced hard at home today and managed to perform the first half of the poomsae. It was also Yash's birthday, and we had a lot of fun.

Day 21:

In today's class, Coach Sir taught us how to count from 1-10 in Korean language, which is Hanna, Dool, Set, Net, Dasut, Yosut, Ill Gop, Yo Dol, A-Hoop, Yoal.

Day 22:

Coach Sir taught white belt students how to do blocks (Makki) and punches (Jireuki), which are simple. However, I am still struggling with kicks. I have been learning only one kick since I joined the class, but I still can't get it right every time.

Day 23:

Due to a school function, I came home late and couldn't attend the class.

I practiced at home instead.

Day 24:

There are ten belts in total till the Black belt, which are White Belt, Yellow Belt, Yellow-1 Belt, Green Belt, Green-1 Belt, Blue Belt, Blue-1 Belt, Red Belt, Red-1 Belt, and Black Belt.

Day 25:

I became good friends with Veer and Rudra in my taekwondo class. They are yellow belts. Veer is excellent at kicking, and Rudra is great at poomsae. Veer will teach me kicking, and Rudra will teach me poomsae. Rudra lives near my house, so he'll teach me all the steps before Coach Sir teaches us. Then coach sir will be surprised by how well I can perform poomsae.

Day-26:

There are a total 8 Poomsae till Black Belt-

Il Jang-Ee Jang-Sam Jang-Sah Jang-Oh Jang-Yook Jang-Chil Jang-Pal Jang.

Day 27:

Today, our class was off, Rudra and I practiced on the terrace of his house.

Day 28:

I fell down while kicking in class today, and the whole class laughed at me. I felt very embarrassed. Coach Sir got angry at the students who were laughing. He motivated me by telling me a joke. I laughed a lot. Coach Sir is a very good person!

Day 29:

"Practice until you're the best. Practice to remain the best."

Day 30:

Now my kick is better, and my legs don't hurt anymore. Sometimes my stomach hurts, though. Coach sir said that if I keep practicing well like this, I can take the belt promotion test, and he will also take me to play matches.

Day 60:

Today I hit 300 kicks non-stop, and Coach sir congratulated me and asked everyone to clap. I don't get bored with taekwondo class anymore; I enjoy going to class. Taekwondo is very interesting. Abhishek and Lucky have been coming to class for three years, and they do 1400-1500 kicks non-stop. My target is to hit equal or more kicks than them. My Poomsae is done now, and I just need to keep revising. My kicks are pretty perfect now. Coach Sir said the belt test would be in one month, and whoever performed best in the white belt would get a trophy. I will get the trophy!

Day 101:

The belt promotion test was conducted today, and I got a trophy and a yellow belt. An external examiner had come for the Belt promotion test. He praised both my kicks and poomsae. Coach Sir and others also congratulated me for getting the trophy. Even after coming home, my mom and I told all the neighbors. Everyone appreciated me. Dad came home in the evening and brought sweets for everyone. Mom and Dad put my photo and trophy on their status, and many people replied and congratulated me. I will not stop at this. I will practice a lot more and get a gold medal by playing matches!

"The harder you train, the shorter the fight."

To be continued...

My Notes

www.ingramcontent.com/pod-product-compliance
Lightning Source LLC
LaVergne TN
LVHW061345080526
838199LV00094B/7369